~How To~

Buy a New Car Like you Practically Stole it

A Step by step guide to buying a new car at a ridiculously low price

How to Buy a New Car Like You Practically Stole It!

Copyright © 2008 Integrity Arts, LLC

All rights reserved. No part of this book may be reproduced in any form or by any means without written permission from the publisher except in the case of brief quotations embodied in critical articles and reviews that include the title of the book and names of the author and publisher.

ISBN 978-0-6152-1738-3

Table of Contents

About this Book 5

About Car Dealers 9

Dealer tricks and fraud. 14

Guiding principles 18

The car dealer's secret techniques. 19

Sleazy Sam's Car Sales Training Manual 20

The Program 30

Conclusion 53

Appendix A - Forms 55

Appendix B - Resources 57

About this Book

This book is for anyone who HATES the car buying experience. It is for those of you who have felt humiliated, ripped-off or just plain aggravated whenever you've shopped for a car.

This book is primarily about purchasing new cars. Although some of the advice can be used towards buying a used car, keep in mind that a used car is an entirely different type of purchase. The primary problem with buying a used car is that one can never accurately assess its value without knowing its history, and the *true* history of a used car is almost impossible to discover. This drastically affects the negotiation process, more often than not, leaving the buyer at a disadvantage. When you purchase a new car, however, you are buying a standard that can easily be compared from dealership to dealership.

I don't buy used cars. I've been burned too many times. By using the system in this book, you'll be able to bring down the price of a new car to within a small difference of a used car. Here is an example.

In this example, we'll look at a used 2006 Toyota Camry LE [*1]

And compare it to a new 2008 Toyota Camry LE

	USED	NEW
Miles	15,000	5
Sticker Price	N/A	22,390 [*5]
Price	17,998 [*1]	19,569 (negotiated) [*6]
Tax	539.94 (NC 3% use tax)	587.05 (3% NC use tax)
DMV	83 (minimum) [*2]	83
Rebate	0	-1000
Documentation	$149 [*3]	0 (negotiated out)
Mileage Adjustment	+1,740 [*4]	0
Total Cost	20,509.94	19,239.05

[*1] Comparison car is Carmax Charlotte Location stock # 4748144 found on 3/5/08

[*2] Carmax NC: minimum 3/5/08

[*3] Carmax NC: 3/5/08

[*4] Mileage adjustment is based on 150,000 mile life of vehicle at which point assumed residual value will be 10% of the original MSRP. Using this calculation, the total value of the vehicle depreciated is divided by the lifetime mileage to arrive at the cost of depreciation per mile: (19,569[a very good negotiated price] − 2200[residual value] = 17,369 [depreciated value] / 150,000 miles = 11.6 cents depreciation cost per mile) .11.6 * 15,000 = $1740 − Please not that this does not include additional costs such a maintenance incurred over the depreciation period.

[*5] Kelley Blue Book 3/19/08 for zip code 27612 with all applicable NC charges.

[*6] Invoice price minus 3% assumed dealer holdback profit.

Now which car would you choose: The used car with a questionable history or the brand new current model for $1270 less? This book will save you thousands on your new car purchase if you follow my advice step by step.

You will learn a bit about how car dealerships operate and a lot about negotiation. By the time you've finished reading, you'll have the tools you need to walk confidently into a new car dealership and walk out with the car of your dreams and some leftover cash.

Let's get started!

About Car Dealers

Who is the car dealer (or salesperson)? What is he like? Does he sleep in a coffin? Does he drink blood? Does he turn into a bat at night and fly into the bedroom of unsuspecting victims? Hardly. Though you wouldn't know it from some of the car dealership horror stories you hear from family and friends.

A car salesperson is a human being who is trying to make a living just like you and me. Car dealers have the same needs and wants as any human being. They want to be liked. They want to feel important. They desire empathy, friends, stress relief and an ego boost. If you provide them with these things you will be a whole lot more successful than if you are combative and hostile.

Joe Bagodonuts is shopping at a Mercury dealership for a new car. After a test drive and a bit of negotiations, Freddy Mercury, his salesman returns to the desk and says

"Mr. Bagodonuts, we were able to get your payment down to $369 per month." Joe replies, "I TOLD YOU I WOULDN'T PAY MORE THAN $299 PER MONTH YOU IDIOT, NOW GO BACK IN THERE AND TALK TO YOUR MANAGER AGAIN OR I'M LEAVING!!!"

Now Freddy has been dealing with this kind of hostility all day, so what do you think his reaction is? He thinks to himself as he walks away, "This guy's a real creep, and likely to slam me on his buyer's survey. I'll go have a cola out back and tell him I couldn't make the deal, and oh look! There's a little old lady looking at a brand new Cougar. ChaChing!"

Car dealers are also in the business to make money. If they did not, you would have a hard time finding the car you need when you need it. The fact that every major city has a dozen or so car dealerships is a convenience and an asset to you. It creates competition, which promotes lower prices and better customer service. It benefits you when they make money...*some* money. Despite this, you should always keep this fact in mind when shopping for a car: The car salesperson, though he may be a great father and husband, a church member and an active part of Kiwanis, is a pure predator on the job. His purpose is to get you to pay as much money for the vehicle as he can squeeze out of you. Many will lie, and defraud in order to meet their objective, some will not.

Do this bit of research: Open the want ads in your local newspaper and turn to the Sales section. You will see ads for car salespeople for almost every dealership in town. If you check weekly, you will see the same ads from the same dealerships. Why? Because the turnover rate for car salesmen is astronomical. Very few can handle the pressure. Even fewer can do it well enough to make sufficient money at it.

You're attitude should be the same as that of the car salesperson. You are there to get every last penny out of the deal that you can. Let them worry about their profit and you worry about your savings. Make no mistake about it: They do not want you to that car away without making money on the deal. Likewise, you should not sign the paperwork before they meet your price.

Dealership's profit

Dealerships make most of their money from a new car sale in 6 ways they are:
- **The profit margin from the sale price of the car**
- **Junk fees**
- **The profit from your trade-in**
- **Commissions and shared profit from financing**
- **Extras such as warranties and add-on features**
- **The holdback or manufacturer's volume bonus and Dealership Incentives**

Let's look at these item by item:

The profit margin: Simply the difference between the price you pay and the price the dealership pays the manufacturer. In the business, this and junk fees are referred to as "front end" money. All the rest is referred to as "back end" money. Your goal will be to eliminate this altogether.

Junk Fees: These are sometimes called "doc fees", "prep fees" or other such nonsense. I'll show you how to do an end run around all of these fees and cut them entirely out of the equation.

The profit from your trade-in: This is the difference between the price the dealership pays you for your old car and the price they sell it for – either on their lot, or at auction. Your goal will be to eliminate this as well because you should NEVER trade in a vehicle. It is a source of loss for you and a possible invitation to fraud at unscrupulous dealerships.

Commissions and shared profit from financing: Whenever you finance through a dealership, they profit and you lose. You lose because rates and terms are generally worse than those you will find through a lending institution and because financing can be an invitation to fraud at unscrupulous dealerships. In any case, they gain leverage over negotiations with you when you are borrowing money from them. Proverbs 22:7 "The rich rules over the poor,
   And the borrower becomes the lender's slave."

Extras such as warranties and add-on features: Extended warranties generally do NOT pay off in the long run. They are structured so that you essentially pay now for repairs that *might* be needed when you are least likely to need them. However, it is my opinion that an extended warranty is a reasonable purchase to protect you from unaffordable repairs if you don't pay too much for the warranty itself. $1,000.00 is the most I'd for a bumper-to-bumper extended warranty to cover your new car to 100,000 miles. Dealerships make huge markups on these, so beware.

The holdback or manufacturer's volume bonus and dealership incentives: This is a volume bonus given to dealerships. It is a substantial source of profit for them. How much of this amounts to per car is only known to the dealership, and varies from dealership to dealership and year to year. For non – luxury brands, this is generally 2% - 3% of the base MSRP, total MSRP or Invoice, depending on the brand. Luxury manufacturers generally offer less incentive to the dealership. In addition, manufacturers offer incentives to dealerships from time to time. These are usually offered on slow moving or highly competitive vehicle types. This is another "secret" source of revenue.

A word about makes and models

Just as clothing goes in and out of fashion, so do car makes and models. There was a time where you would have been thought to be crazy to buy a Chrysler product. That was until Lee Iacocca resurrected the brand name. Likewise, different manufacturers lead the way in the various classes of vehicle. Chrysler had long held the lead in minivans until the Honda Odyssey and Toyota Sienna began winning consumer and safety awards. Ford's lead in trucks began to slip when Dodge re-designed their Ram line into a massive chrome infused road monster. Since Toyota was one of the first manufacturers with a practical hybrid (the Prius), they took the lead with this type of vehicle.

What do these ever changing popularity contests mean to you the buyer?

Simply put, your ability to negotiate a winning deal is inversely proportional to the popularity of the vehicle. In other words, you will not be able to negotiate a very good deal for the "Newly re-designed, 5 star crash rated, consumer's journal best-buy, every mom must have one, minivan" as you would with the "ugly duckling, soon to be discontinued, wood side panel, autumn brown station wagon." Again, let's use Toyota's Prius as an example. When gasoline hit $3.50 per gallon, people were literally lining up to get them. Some dealerships were even charging a markup above the sticker price. Imagine trying to negotiate in that environment. Your efforts would go nowhere. In general, however, most cars are VERY negotiable, and you will rarely have to pay more than the invoice price for the car if you negotiate properly.

What about "No Haggle Pricing"?

No Haggle Pricing is a fairly new phenomenon that is sold to the consumer as a way to get a great deal on a vehicle without the hassle of negotiating with a salesperson. Remember, most people *hate* the negotiation process. In reality, the dealership is adding a comfortable profit margin into the front-end of the deal. When it comes to the back-end (financing, warrantees, trade-ins) you'll find that you still have to weave your way around a maze of high-pressure sales tactics! Don't fall for this one. By carefully following my program, you'll practically eliminate their back-end margin and shave their front-end to a bare minimum.

Dealer tricks and fraud.

An entire book can be written about this topic. I will only touch upon a few well-known traps and give you some general principles to work by so you can avoid being scammed.

As far as I'm concerned, there are two general categories: Crimes and Sleaze. Sometimes the line between the two is somewhat blurry.

Crimes

Simply put, crimes are those things that are punishable by law. On the less serious end of this spectrum are those things that can be considered general consumer complaints: Bait and switch, false advertising and other deceptive business practices. These are bad for you for obvious reasons, but are easy to avoid if you are careful in your negotiations and dealings. For starters: never believe a single word of dealership advertising. The only purpose of any dealership advertising is to get you in the door to test-drive *their* car. Secondly, do not take anything they say seriously until you see it on paper, *really* seriously when you complete all documentation with a business manager.

On the more dangerous side are things that can really ruin your day: Selling a used car as new. Verbally stating one thing while you sign a totally different deal. Offering to pay off a trade vehicle and never doing it. Credit and identity theft. The list goes on.

Can you guarantee that you will avoid all of theses scams? No. Can you guaranty that your house will not be broken into? No. You can only take measures to protect yourself.

Start by talking to friends and neighbors. Make inquiries into your attorney general's office and the local Better Business bureau. Generally, large big name multi-dealership chains have much more to lose than the small single dealership and will tend to have standard business practices to protect their reputations. On the other hand, a small town family owned dealership that has been in business for decades has a reputation to protect and in most cases will do business honorably. Choose carefully.

Be absolutely sure to read every document passed before you. Don't let the salesperson try to rush you through this. Read both the back AND front of every piece of paper. If in doubt, DO NOT SIGN.

Sleaze

Here's a list of things to watch out for:

The "four square" – a confusing jumble of number to trick you into paying more. You will avoid this by negotiating for the price of the car ONLY.

"You have to buy an extended warranty, or the bank won't finance you" This is ALWAYS a lie.

"We don't take checks from online lenders. They all bounce" They will offer you their financing at a higher rate. This is another lie.

"This is Jim the salesman who sold you your new Gremlin last week. Unfortunately, your financing fell through, but we were able to get you a new deal at a pretty good rate. Just come in and write a check for 1,100 dollars to cover the difference" This is called spot delivery. You will avoid this by NEVER financing through a dealership.

"The Federal Government requires you to provide your social security number on this form (credit application) because of the Patriot Act." This is a lie to get you to fill out a credit application so they can sell you their own lousy credit products. You never have to provide this information since you will NEVER finance through the dealership

"This car has traction control or other feature" (no, it's only available on a pricier model). Another sleazy sales tactic. Do your research.

"We lost the key to your trade-in car" (delay) This wears you out and gives them negotiating power.

"You poor credit score (lie) only qualifies you for the 9.9% financing, not the 2.9% we advertised." Another lie.

"Hi, I'm the general manager, what can we do for you today?" This is known as the takeover or T.O. You will have to restart negotiations anew. This is a delaying tactic designed to break your will.

"What is the maximum payment you can make?" This will tell them exactly how much they can get out of you.

"We can allow a lower down payment, but the money's got to come from somewhere, your payment will rise." Dealerships love this. They make more on high payments than anything else. Just don't finance with a dealership!

"We can get you into this car for only $299 per month." They entice you with a low payment while you're really paying a higher overall price.

"We just sold the car you were looking at online, but we have another just like it." This is a type of bait and switch.

"That's the documentation fee, everyone pays it." You won't!

"That invoice price you found in your research is wrong, we really paid this for the vehicle." Don't buy it. Sometimes discrepancies do exist between the actual invoice and those that you will find in your research. Since you have no way of knowing the actual amounts, go with the lower figure – you can be sure that they will never tell you they paid LESS for the vehicle!

Keep all of these tactics in mind. The way to beat the dealership on all of these is to follow the plan outlined below step by step.

Guiding principles

Never trade a car.

Never use dealership financing.

Don't be a payment buyer. Resist the temptation when the salesperson tells you that he can "get you in this car for only $249 per month"

Choose your make, model and options before even trying to negotiate

Do your research ahead of time.

Be friendly.

Be persistent.

Stay in control of the process.

Don't let your emotions get the best of you.

Be patient – the process can take weeks. Expect to walk away more than once.

Never let on how much you really like the car.

Never believe anything a cars salesperson tells you – verify everything.

Try not to let on that you will not be financing through them.

Keep your minimum and maximum prices in mind.

The only offer you negotiate on is an "Out the door price" or O.T.D.

Never pay more than 1,000 for a complete bumper-to-bumper extended warranty to 100,000 miles.

The car dealer's secret techniques.

Before you go into a dealership to negotiate a price on your new creampuff, you've got to know how they operate. This section is a stylized version of the typical dealership's training manual. I felt it was best to present it to you in this manner to give you as much information as possible in a short format. I've taken the liberty to spell out some of the things that you would have to "read between the lines" to understand as well as some things that do not appear in a training manual but are communicated verbally to each salesperson. Read it carefully. I guaranty you'll see it played out before you when you go for your test drive. In some cases even word for word.

Now for a bit of role-playing: Assume you're the rookie salesperson as you read this section. It will facilitate your understanding of how they operate.

Sleazy Sam's Car Sales Training Manual

Your Objectives.

1. Always be in control of the sales process. You lead while the customer follows.
2. Get the customer to like you.
3. Get the customer to drive the car.
4. Get the customer to sit down at the bargaining table.

Most customers will buy a car within 48 – 72 hours of first walking on the lot of a dealership. This means you have one opportunity to sell them a car. If they don't buy from you today, they probably will not come back.

Your first goal: Assist the customer in finding the right car. Qualify them for financing.

1. Greet the customer with a friendly hello. Use this script: "Welcome to Sleazy Sam's Edsel. I'm _____, your product specialist. My goal is to help you find the right car for your needs. What would you like to drive today?"
2. While discussing models, ask them if they know how they will be paying for the car and what they will be trading. Ask them what their current monthly payment is and who their finance company is. This will give you a good idea of their creditworthiness. If they mention that they are financing through "A, B, or C" *[Authors note: these are lenders that specialize in bad credit cases]* get them to fill out a credit

application right away before you waste any time with someone unqualified to purchase. If they have a trade, offer them a free appraisal. Get the keys for their trade, and have the used car department begin the appraisal.

NEVER negotiate until after the test drive and after they express their desire to purchase the vehicle.

If at any point in the process, the customer objects, acknowledge their objection, and proceed with the sales process undaunted.

Common objections and your reply:

Customer: "I'm just looking"

You: "Great, take your time, let's look at these Model Ts over here. Follow me."

Customer: "How much will you take off the sticker price?"

You: "I don't have all the figures right here, let's go for a test drive and then we can discuss the price. Follow me."

Customer: "How much can I get for my 1934 LaSalle?"

You: "That's up to the used car appraisal department. While they work on it, let's look at a few Corvairs. Follow me."

In each case, the phrase "Follow me", establishes your control over the process. After uttering the phrase "follow me", begin walking to the car lot. Do not look back. The customer will always follow.

Your second goal: Build excitement.

After you lead the customer to a car of his or her preference, obtain the keys from the key room and open up all doors and the hood. Begin at the driver side, and show all the features the car has to offer.

Speak quickly and build excitement. Lead the customer clockwise around the car pointing out each feature as you go. Put special emphasis on safety features as most customers identify safety as a prime selling point. *[Author's note: All dealerships have a book that describes the advantages of their cars. Ironically, the same company produces these books for each manufacturer. If manufacturer A's minivan has the best side crash rating, manufacturer B's minivan might have the best rear impact rating. These are all listed in their respective books]*

Have the customer sit in the passenger seat. Start the car while you point out a few interior features. Controlling the process, instruct the passenger to close his door and drive to the test drive area. The customer may be caught by surprise, but will always go along with the test drive that is now underway.

Your third goal: Build rapport.

After the customer takes the wheel, you will want to slow things down a bit. Allow them to enjoy the car. Ask them what they will be using the car for. Share a personal story or two. Get to know them and allow them to know you. This rapport allows you to build trust and makes it more difficult for them to oppose their newfound friend when negotiations get underway.

Always remain in control during the test drive. Tell them where to go, where to stop, where to turn etc.

Go for the "20 Yeses": Ask the customer numerous questions to which they will answer "yes". Try to get 20 Yeses' out of them. Possible questions are: "Do you like the visibility?", "Does the radio sound good?" "Is the seat position comfortable?"

By doing this, you build a positive image of the car in the customer's mind. *[Authors note: These repeated affirmations are actually a form of hypnosis!]*

At the end of the test drive, have the customer pull the car into the "sold car spot" in from of the showroom. This will build an image of ownership in the customer's mind.

Ask the customer: "Do you like the car?"

If they reply "yes": "If I've earned your business today, let's go inside and see what we can do about getting you a great deal."

If they reply "no": Write down the stock number of the car and offer to show them another car

Negotiations:

After taking the customer inside and taking their contact information, tell them you will speak to your manager and see what kind of deal you can work out for them.

Fill out a deal sheet with the car's stock number. Your manager will fill out an offer sheet. The offer sheet is arranged in the "four square" configuration (See figure below).

Trade – In	Car Price
1997 Ford Probe [1] $1,375	2008 Import SUV 4-Door SE [2] 36, 245 -4,000 (rebate) 32,245
Down Payment 6,100	**Monthly payment** 60 months 514.18 [3]

[Author's footnotes:

1. Trade in is a 1997 Ford Probe with 132,000 miles in good condition. Kelley Blue Book Trade-in value for zip code 27615 as of 5/9/2008.
2. Purchased car price is based on Kelley Blue Book MSRP as of 5/9/2008. Though this is an actual brand and model, the brand and model were chosen arbitrarily and in no way represents the actual business practices of any manufacturer or dealership.
3. Payment amount is based on $24,770 financed at 9% for 60 months

]

In the top left corner is the price we will pay for their trade-in.

In the upper right corner is the price of the vehicle. This will always start as the *sticker price* minus any rebates.

In the bottom left corner is the down payment at 20% of the balance.

In the lower right corner is the calculated monthly payment.

We arrived at this deal in the following way:

The trade-in value is the minimum value determined by the used car department.

The vehicle price always starts at the sticker price of the car. A rebate is included in this box.

The down payment always starts at 20% of the balance due.

The monthly payment is the high end of what we feel the customer will be willing to pay based on your initial interview. In this case, the customer may have said they were looking for a monthly payment of no more than $399 per month. We will choose something over $500 per month because we always want to stretch them out of their comfort zone and allow room to negotiate. A loan will be chosen to match that payment amount.

Most customers will have the following reaction to the deal sheet.
1. They will scoff at the trade-in value of their car.
2. The will let you know that the down payment is too high for them to afford.
3. They will totally ignore the price of the car. *[Authors note: This is still at the sticker price!]*

4. They will be shocked and disappointed at the monthly payment amount, paying little attention to term or interest rates.

This presentation will change the mood of negotiation at this point. From this position of shock, we will be able to bring the price down to a point where the dealership makes a profit and the customer feels as if he or she is getting a good deal. Your role now is to be their advocate and "see what you can do for them"

Your response to the above customer reactions should be as follows:

1. If they object to the value of their trade-in car:

Tell them that this is a fair appraisal based on the condition of the car, and that we as a dealership have to make a profit when we re-sell it. If they continue to object, tell them you will speak to your manager about getting a better price for them.

2. If they express an objection to the down payment:

Tell them that a 20% down payment is standard, and that we can certainly accept a lower down payment, but that will raise their monthly payment.

3. If they express an objection to the sticker price of the car:

Tell them that this is the manufacturer's suggested retail price of the car that the federal government requires to be posted on every new vehicle. Move quickly on to the monthly payment box. A suggested dialogue would go like this: "That's the manufacturers suggested retail price as mandated by the federal government. Are you comfortable with this monthly payment?"

In most cases, the customer will follow your lead to the monthly payment. If the customer insists on a discount off of the sticker price, tell them that you'll speak to your manager about it.

4. If they express an objection to the monthly payment:

Tell them the length of the loan and interest rate, only if they ask.

Ask them what they'd like to pay (as if you forgot what they originally said). Offer to speak to your manager about it.

As you depart to speak to your manager, quickly return as if you forgot something and ask the customer: "If I can't get your monthly payment, what is the maximum you'll pay per month?" Their reply will give you their maximum figure.

This entire process is a type of "good cop – bad cop" scenario. At this point, the customer sees you as his advocate. Don't forget to re-enforce this when speaking to your customer. Phrase your sentences as follows: "I'll try to get you a better trade-In price." "Let me see if I can get you a better monthly payment."

When you return to your manager, the following will take place:

You will explain their areas of objection to your manager. Your manager will adjust the down payment if requested by the customer. If the customer requests a lower payment or higher trade-in price, your manager may give in somewhat if he feels it will get them closer to closing a deal. Any request to adjust the sticker price will be delayed.

This exchange may be repeated more than once. If your customer attempts to negotiate after two meetings with your manager, your manager will give you a "take over" or T.O. He or she will step in and take over negotiations.

A T.O. can also be used if a customer becomes irate, threatens to leave, or if your relationship with the customer deteriorates in any way.

The T.O. achieves a number of objectives: The customer has to re-establish a relationship with someone new, thus tiring them out. *[Authors note: The entire sales process is designed to take from 3 to 4 hours with the intent of tiring you out. Very few customers are ambivalent about the purchase by the time they start negotiating. After the test drive, most people desperately want the car. Stretching out the process reduces the customer's desire to negotiate further.]*

The T.O. also allows a new relationship to be established if your relationship with the customer has gone sour.

The T.O. has a high intimidation factor.

When your customer finally agrees to a deal, they will sign the deal sheet and proceed to the business manager. At this time, they will be offered a number warranty options, sign the final paperwork and close the deal.

If the customer is bringing their own financing, the business manager will work towards convincing them to switch to a dealership finance product. This may be a lengthy process. Take this time to ensure that the car is properly prepped.

If the customer objects at this point to any of the doc or prep fees, they will simply be told that these are standard fees paid by everyone.

Delivery: After the papers are signed and the keys are handed over, it will be your responsibility to explain each feature of the new vehicle to the customer. See them off and be sure to ask for a referral.

[Authors note: As you can see, the process is designed to keep you at a disadvantage, wear you down and get you to commit to their terms while they retain control of the transaction.

Here is a breakdown of the dealership's profit in the preceding example:

The profit margin from the sale price of the car	$3,330 [1]
The profit from sale of your trade-in	$2,685 [2]
Shared profit from financing	$1,422.53 [3]
Extras such as warranties and add-on features	$900 [4]
The holdback or manufacturer's volume bonus	$1,087.35 [5]
Dealer incentives	$2,000 [6]
Junk fees	$399
Total	$11,823.88 [7]

[Authors footnotes:

1. Purchased car profit price is based on Kelley Blue Book MSRP of an unnamed import SUV minus invoice as of 5/9/2008.

2. Trade in profit is based on retail value for 1997 Ford Probe with 132,000 miles in good condition from Kelley Blue Book for zip code 27615

3. Financing profit is based on 2% difference between what a dealership might pay for a loan (9%) and what they might re-sell it for (7%) on the financed amount of $24,770

4. Assumes a warranty purchased by the dealership for $600 and re-sold to the customer at $1,500.

5. Assumes a dealership holdback of 3% based on the MSRP.

6. Assumes dealership incentive equal to ½ of the consumer rebate incentive.

7. As you can see, assumptions were made based on common practices. It is the author's intent to provide a realistic example of potential profit on the sale of the typical vehicle. This is not meant to represent the practices of a particular manufacturer or dealership. In addition, cost and price structures are subject to change at any time.
]

Now that you know how they operate, your job will be to resist and bypass their tactics at every turn. As you will see, this will be very easy, and **rewarding**]

The Program

This program is intended to give you a simple step-by-step method of purchasing a car for the lowest possible price. You should follow each step exactly.

Before you begin, I want to remind you of an important fact. As you noticed in the preceding chapter, dealerships have designed their system to take advantage of the payment buyer. They make a tremendous amount of money from the typical payment buyer. Payment buyers are abundant. If they don't sell the car to you, they are quite sure that a sucker will come along soon enough and purchase on the payment plan. They are right. This will limit the amount of money they are willing to lose on you! Nevertheless, if you follow the program correctly, in most cases, you will have a firm agreement before they know that you will not be financing through them.

Step one: Choosing the right car

If you don't already know the make and model of the car you want, you should have some idea of what you'd like your car to do. It may be something to get you to and from work, or something to haul the kids and their sports equipment around town. Whatever the case, do your research ahead of time and settle on a make, model *and* options before you visit a car dealership's lot. The Internet is an excellent resource for this. Most every manufacturer's website allows you to peruse all of their models and options. Sites like Edmunds (www.edmunds.com) have excellent reviews and owner comments to help guide you.

A word on timing:

This is also a good time to determine when the new model year starts for the make and model you are interested in. Researching this will help you know the best time to shop. Generally, dealerships are quite desperate to clear their inventories in the month prior to the new model year's arrival. For example, if the new AMC Pacer comes out in September, late August will be the optimum time to buy. Always start your purchase process about 1 week prior to the end of each month. Dealers have quotas and are often very motivated to make deals at the end of each month. Starting out one week in advance gives you time to negotiate.

Eventually, you'll want to test drive the car you have in mind. A used car superstore like Carmax will have most makes and models available for you to test drive. Since they strive to create a low-pressure environment, you can test drive cars all day long without much hassle.

Another way to try out the car you're interested in is to look for want ads from individuals selling similar cars used. Give them a call and go for a test drive or two.

Know any friends who own the car you have in mind? Pick their brains and drive their cars.

Step Two: Pricing your car.

After you've determined your make, model and options, you'll want to determine your maximum negotiated price for your car. You'll remember, this is the invoice price of the car, plus Tax Title and Tags (TTT) minus any rebate being offered. Both Edmunds (www.edmunds.com) and Kelley Blue Book (www.kbb.com) are excellent resources for this. Follow the various screens for new car pricing to determine your invoice price. This is region dependent, so be sure to properly enter the location where you intend to purchase the vehicle. Look at the manufacturer's website for any rebate. Call your local motor vehicle office to determine the cost of any applicable taxes, the cost to transfer title, and the price of new tags. Here is an example of such a calculation:

2008 Ford F150 Supercab 4 door XL 2wd Automatic [1]

Invoice Price : 23,285.00

Rebate: -3,000

Tax: 608.55 [2]

DMV: 83 [3]

Maximum Negotiated Price: 20,976.55

1. For zip code 27615 as per Kelley Blue Book 5/13/08
2. 3% NC use tax
3. NC minimum DMV costs for title and plate

Now, keep in mind that this is the **maximum** price you will pay unless purchasing a highly demanded vehicle.

Next, search the Internet for information on dealership cash. This is the "secret" incentive that manufacturers offer to dealerships to move a certain make and model. Also known as "manufacturer to dealer incentives", this can be one of the most difficult numbers to uncover. Often sales managers will even keep this figure secret from their own sales staff. My advice here is to take the following approach:

1. Do some networking. Ask questions on a forum such as "Yahoo Answers (answers.yahoo.com). You never know when you'll come across someone who has the answers you're looking for.

2. Look through your local newspaper. Take note of radio, TV and Internet ads in your area. If your car is one of the top 3 most heavily promoted cars by the same manufacturer AND has a consumer rebate, assume there is a manufacturer's rebate. A good rule of thumb is to calculate the manufacturer's incentive as ½ of the current consumer rebate.

Calculating the dealership holdback can be a bit tricky. This varies by the volume of cars a dealership sells. You can roughly calculate this to be between 2% and 4% of the base MSRP, total MSRP or Invoice depending on the dealership. Luxury brands generally offer less to the dealership in the way of holdback. I like to go with a higher figure when calculating my minimum price. Include the holdback and dealership cash as *negatives* in the above calculation. This gives you your **minimum** negotiated price. Here is an example of this calculation:

> 2008 Ford F150 Supercab 4 door XL 2wd Automatic [1]
>
> Invoice Price : 23,285.00
>
> Rebate: -3,000
>
> Dealer Cash: -1,500 [2]
>
> Dealership Holdback: - 997.8 [3]
>
> Tax: 533.62 [4]
>
> DMV: 83 [5]
>
> **Minimum Negotiated Price:** 18,403.82
>
> 1. For zip code 27615 as per Kelley Blue Book 5/13/08
>
> 2. Dealer cash is estimated as ½ of the consumer rebate
>
> 3. Dealership holdback is calculated as 4% of MSRP (24,945 KBB 5/13/08)
>
> 4. 3% NC use tax
> 5. NC minimum DMV costs for title and plate

I call this the minimum price because quite frankly, a dealership loses money when pricing a car below this level. The only time that a dealer will venture into this territory is when he:

a)   Is assured of making some back-end money.

b)   Is selling a damaged vehicle as new.

c)   Has a real dog on his lot that he'd rather lose money on than look at another day.

As you can see these are rare circumstances, and in reality, the price you're able to negotiate will be somewhere between your minimum and maximum prices.

Step Three: Finding financing.

Remember, you will not be going to the dealership for financing. This may seem like bad advice in light of some of the very low dealership interest rates that crop up from time to time. Keep in mind that whenever you see a 0%, 1.9% or 2.9% loan, that these are usually very short term loans (3 years is the usual maximum) and only buyers with very high credit scores qualify. Quite frankly, most of the people who can afford to get into one of these loans can usually afford to pay for the car outright. In addition, most of these offers are in lieu of a manufacturer's rebate. So for example, you might see a deal like this: "1.9 % financing *or* $3,000 cash back." And of course the small print would read something like this: "1.9% financing is only available on loans of 48 month or less and requires a 780 beacon score or better". Take the cash. In almost every circumstance, the cash rebate saves you more money than the lower interest rate.

So where do you go for financing? Your first stop should be your local credit union. Credit unions exist to serve their members rather than stockholders. If you don't belong to a credit union, ask your employer if they are affiliated with a credit union. If not, wholesale clubs, fraternal organizations and even religious organizations are often affiliated with a credit union you can join by opening a checking or savings account with a modest initial balance.

If you cannot join a credit union, try financing online. Outfits such as Lending Tree (www.lendingtree.com) and BankRate.com (www.bankrate.com) will allow you to see rates offered by competing banks. If you have poor credit be sure to try a lender that specializes in credit problems like Wells Fargo Financial (http://financial.wellsfargo.com). In any case, an online lender will provide you with a "blank check" if you're approved. It is valid for a dollar amount in the range in which you were approved. So, for example, you might have been approved for up to thirty thousand dollars, and the check they provide you with will be valid for the 25,000 price you negotiate on your new car.

Step 4: Selling Your Old Car.

In keeping with the principles we set out previously, you will not be trading your car to the dealership under any circumstance. You will sell the car yourself instead.

The first step you should take is to find the value of your car. Again, this is easily done using such online pricing guides as Edmunds (www.edmunds.com) or Kelley Blue Book (www.kbb.com). They both offer step-by-step guides to determining the value of your used vehicle. Being honest with yourself about the condition of your car will provide you with the most accurate figures. You will want to note 3 values for your vehicle, they are

a) The private party value – or the amount you can get for your vehicle in a private sale.

b) The retail value of your car – The amount a dealership will ask for your car when they resell it.

c) The trade in value of your car – The amount a dealership will give you in a trade in.

What do these figures mean to you? The trade-in value of your car represents the average price a dealership will give you for your car. This is going to be the lowest of the 3 figures. You will use this for reference only. The Retail value of the car is usually the highest figure and represents the price a dealer would sell a used car for. The private party value should be about what you can get for your car when selling through a newspaper ad. Pricing your car at the retail value and allow yourself to be "negotiated down" to the private party value is a good strategy that will give a win-win feeling to your buyer and provide you with a fair price when selling in a private sale.

When selling your car yourself, you should consider how much hassle you are willing to tolerate. Selling your own car can be a real drag if done the old fashioned way (newspaper ad). Fortunately, today we have a few other options open to us. For one, you can post an ad online for free (in most locations) using Craigslist (www.craigslist.com). You can also place a listing on Ebay and generate a large amount of interest. When selling online, beware of some of the various scams being pulled on car sellers. Ebay has an excellent guide to protecting yourself from such fraudulent transactions. You can find it at (http://pages.ebay.com/securitycenter/).

Whether by newspaper, Craigslist, Ebay or some other advertising venue, you will have to show the car yourself and negotiate on your own. This involves an amount of personal interaction that you may not feel comfortable with. If you'd rather not take this route, another option is to sell your car to a dealership. In this case, you will price your vehicle somewhere between the trade-in and private party values you previously researched. Carmax (www.carmax.com) is an excellent outlet for this. They tend to offer prices in exactly this range and make the selling process simple.

When selling in a private sale (to an individual), you must obtain the title to your existing car if you haven't already. Do not let a dealership pay off your loan. This has been a source of heartache to many a seller. Some unscrupulous dealers will offer to do so, and then deny it later, leaving you with the bill. If you must pay off an existing loan, and have the cash to do so, now is the time to do it. If you don't already have the cash to do it, ask about including your payoff amount in your new car loan. Some lenders will allow you to do so. If you are "upside down" on your loan (your loan balance is more than you can get for the car) you have a difficult situation on your hands. You will have to scrape up some of the cash yourself to make up this difference.

Step Five: The Test Drive.

So you've done all your homework and now your ready to make the big purchase and save thousands while doing it. First off, I want to remind you of one important fact to put things in perspective: The test drive is actually part of the negotiation process, a process that can take weeks. Keep that in mind as you prepare to take what can often seem like a roller coaster ride.

Before you actually take that fateful journey to one of the car dealerships you've selected, you'll want to choose the actual car you will purchase. This can be done with ease on the Internet. Most manufacturers have an "inventory search" feature right on their website. You can enter your zip code and search for the model and options of your choosing. Most sites will give you a list of cars, dealerships where they are located and a downloadable image of the actual window sticker with VIN! You should use this to pick out the exact car you want. Note the VIN for your visit to the dealership. Following this with a visit to the Edmunds or Kelley Blue Book website should give you the exact invoice price for that car. Be sure to calculate your minimum and maximum prices before you proceed (see Appendix A for worksheets). When you've done this, you're ready to test drive the exact car you wish to buy and have exact figures on the very same vehicle. When using a manufacturer's website, you will often be presented with the option of contacting the dealership. If you do so, you will be put in contact with the dealership's "internet sales" department. Having recognized the impact of the Internet, most dealerships have set up a system to catch the sale immediately, before you even walk into a showroom. Many will even negotiate a price on the vehicle over the phone. This can be a useful tool for you, and I'll show you how to use to your advantage later in this chapter, but I recommend making at least one visit to a dealership. There are a few reasons for this. First, despite negotiating over the phone, you have NOT agreed to a deal until you pay, sign the paperwork and drive off. Some unscrupulous dealerships will even tempt you with a lowball rate that they do not intend to honor. I've even seen dealerships shut down a deal after the paperwork was signed! They'd rather take a chance on being sued than close on the teaser lowball price they quoted you. In such cases, an excuse is usually offered. Such excuses usually sound the same. "We just realized that our leasing department had a contract on that vehicle, it was a mistake to even have that on our lot. We'd like to honor the same offer on another vehicle" [of course no similar vehicle will be found]. Internet sales are not the shortcut they'd like you to believe they are. In all likelihood, you'll have to do some or much of the negotiations once you arrive. Secondly, shopping the dealership first will force the dealership to invest in you. Just as they prolong negotiations in the hope that you won't want to waste your whole afternoon only to lose the deal, the reverse is also true. After spending some time and effort with you the dealership will not want to lose you as a customer. Thirdly, if you can't work out a deal, you will at least have a firm quote in hand with a contact person and vehicle noted. This provides you with bargaining power should you decide to go the Internet route later on.

Now you're ready to head out. Start of with a bit of mental preparation. Remind yourself of a few important facts. Recite these to yourself:

I will not be sold on dealership financing.

I will not change my make model or options.

I will be friendly

I will be persistent

I will not let my emotions get the best of me.

I will be patient.

I will give the impression of ambivalence.

I will remain in control of the process.

I will not believe anything told to me that is not in writing or independently verified.

I will give ambiguous answers to loan questions.

I will keep my Maximum and Minimum prices in mind.

I will only negotiate an "Out the Door" price.

I will never pay more than $1,000 for a 100,000 mile warranty.

As you approach a dealership for a test drive, remember your ambivalence. It sometimes even helps if you portray distaste for the car in question. Try this experiment. Stand in front of a mirror while sucking on a lemon. Remember that face. It will come in handy! Be sure to leave all of your research at home. One of the worst things you can do is arrive with a folder full of facts and figures. It tells a bit too much about your enthusiasm and preparedness.

When you arrive at the dealership, a salesperson or two will approach you. Greet them in a friendly manner. Tell them that you're there to look at car X because you heard it was a good buy or a good performer or whatever ... but you're not sure, you're also looking at brand Y. RELAX. The salesperson is just another person trying to make a living in a grueling environment.

Here's a good ruse, I've used it a number of times myself. "My wife wants car X, but I really like car Y (a different brand). To make her happy, I just want to check it out."

Remember: Ambivalence is the key.

It also helps to be pressed for time. The best time to visit a dealership is on your lunch break. Wear a watch and look at it constantly. Tell your salesperson about your time constraints as soon as she approaches. "I only have a few minutes, but I'd like to check out the new Chevy Vega".

At this point, the salesperson will lead you to a car and will attempt to build excitement, establish control or both.

Your reaction: You're disinterested and doing your own thing. As she's leading you around the car, you're walking in the other direction, climbing in the back seat, or even crawling underneath the vehicle. This may seem rude, and it is, but just remember, the game they're playing with you is far more obnoxious. If the salesperson attempts to take control and lead you around like a puppy, you're walking in the opposite direction. When she utters the phrase "follow me", that's your cue to walk across the lot to another car. This will be maddening to your salesperson, but will establish YOUR control and disinterest.

Your salesperson may want to take you inside to take down your personal information and get a copy of your driver's license before the test drive begins. This is ok. You should comply with this. It is a reasonable request on their part, and will allow them to call you (which they certainly will) if you cannot finalize negotiations at this time.

Prior to the test-drive, your salesperson will attempt to qualify you for credit. They may even ask you outright how you intend to finance the vehicle and how good your credit is. NEVER let on that you will not be financing through them. Answer the questions ambiguously. For example, the salesperson may ask "Have you heard about our low 1.9% rate?" Your answer: "Sounds interesting, I'll have to check that out." If he asks, "How do you intend to pay for this?" You answer: "I'd like to see what you can offer in the way of financing." This in no way commits you to anything but listening to a few rate quotes. The reason for this is to keep them from knowing that you have your own financing and therefore will be denying them a significant source of income.

As you test-drive the vehicle, the salesperson will attempt to slow things down and get personal. He may start out asking you what you intend to use the vehicle for and continue by asking you about your family, kids, job etc. Go with the flow. Counter by asking him personal questions. Ask how long he's been working there. How he deals with the long hours. How his wife deals with the long hours. Having been in the car business, my rap goes something like this: "I really have a lot of respect for you guys. I was in the same shoes as you were, when I worked for Ducky's Datsun down on Main Street and man were those hours long!" This does a few things for me. Firstly, it establishes rapport. Secondly it tells them that I know a few of their tricks. You may not be able to state the same claims, but if you have a friend or relative in the car business, you can use the same line replacing the "I" with "Uncle Vinny" or "My best friend Horatio". If you have any sales experience at all, relating to them on this level is also an excellent way to build rapport.

At this point, you may be asking, "why bother getting personal?" Surely, you can take the same position that you would on a job interview and state that you're interested in the car and not in divulging your personal details, but by doing so you're missing an important opportunity. You see; the salesperson is building rapport for the simple reason that by becoming your friend, he establishes his position as "good cop". It also becomes much more difficult for you to disappoint him. Guess what? The same thing works in reverse! By relating to him and expressing empathy for his difficult position, it becomes very hard for him to disappoint you! He is much more likely to become your advocate. Most people HATE car salespeople. Being the person with empathy puts you in a rare position.

Remember that during the test drive, the salesperson will still attempt to retain control. Requests such as, "Take this exit", "Change lanes", or "Turn on your wipers" should be complied with to the degree that it is safe and reasonable. Don't be bossed around, but don't be unreasonable either.

This is also the time where the salesperson will attempt to obtain the "20 yeses". Each of his questions should be countered with a negative, or ambivalent answer. For example, "Do you like the view" should be countered with "Why is this sun visor so low, it's very annoying".

You will never talk price during the test drive. Salespeople are trained to avoid any such conversation, so it shouldn't be an issue. If it does come up, just sidestep it. When you conclude the test drive the salesperson will generally "ask for the sale" and invite you inside to negotiate. Here's a script to follow before you negotiate:

Salesperson: "If you like the car and I've earned your business, let's see if I can get you a good deal."

You: "I'll think about it. (look at your watch) Let me have your card."

Salesperson: (usually baffled). "Ok no problem. Would you like to drive something else."

You: " I'll let you know" (start to walk. Pause. Look at your watch again, and then shake your head. Look at the sticker on the car again.) "Hold on for a second…

[Author's note: Remember this, It is the single most important line you'll utter in the whole process.]

You: "If you can get me: [your minimum negotiated price], **Out the door**, we can do business today"

Salesperson: "I'll be right back."

[Author's note: A dim witted salesperson might reply with a clever remark such as 'I thought you didn't like it' or some other such nonsense. You're reply is simply to repeat your offer above. Remember to use the phrase 'Out the Door']

At this point, you should not sit down and remember not to relinquish control. You've made it clear that you must leave shortly. Stick to this schedule, it will put pressure on them to negotiate.

There are a few key moves you made in this short transaction: When you asked for his card, you maintained good manners but made it clear that you were not bluffing. Most bluffers usually act with hostility or threats. You were just establishing your control and ambivalence and being mature about it. You are also setting your terms firmly and decisively by asking for an OTD price. You also bypassed many of the junk fees used by dealers to raise the price. You're asking for a final price. If they ask you how you arrived at your offer price, give them a runaround. Tell them that it's basically all the car is worth to you. Never mention the holdback or dealer cash as this is something dealers consider sacred. In general, you should not talk about your calculations or this book! Play your cards close to your vest. Your objective is to avoid arguments and get to their best price.

Step Six: Negotiations:

Making an offer on the car has just brought you to the table to negotiate. The goal of negotiations at this stage is not to buy the car, but to walk away with the best price they can provide so that you can go out and shop other dealerships. In the rare case where you can bring them to your minimum in one visit, BUY THE CAR! In most cases however, your offer will usually bring one of the following reactions:

a) The salesperson will have you wait while he speaks to his manager and will return with a counter offer.

b) The salesperson will ask you to wait while he speaks to his manager and will come back and basically say no, make another offer. This usually sounds something like this; "Let's be realistic, make an offer we can do something with."

In either case, remember this important fact: A dealership will almost NEVER accept your offer. You must accept theirs. This gets back to the control issue. In an effort to maintain control, the dealership will not accept your terms. This is not a problem. You are baiting them to your terms. They will eventually make an offer that will save you thousands and in their mind, will deliver the profit they crave. Here's where they're mistaken: When they agree to a price that's less than or equal to your maximum price, they are relying on the idea that they will get you for some back-end money (financing, warrantees etc.). They will realize this mistake soon enough, but not until you're far enough into the deal to have them by the horns. But first you've got some work to do.

If the dealership comes back with a "no", your job will be to hold out as long as you can before making a counter-offer. Ask them what they will take. They will usually reply with a smart remark such as "a reasonable offer". Shrug your shoulders, act frustrated, start to walk away etc. Things aren't going well at this point, but you should not leave this dealership without a quote. If you must, make a counter-offer at about the 25% between your minimum and maximum prices. Always use the phrase "Out The Door". See if they bite. In a worst case, keep moving up to your maximum. When you finally get them to counter-offer, say thank you, shake hands and walk away. Don't be surprised if they rap on your windshield as you drive off with a better counter-offer. It happens. In any case, be polite, thank them and move on. If it's not your minimum, it's only a comparison offer as far as you're concerned.

On the other hand, if the dealership makes a counter-offer, you'll want to get right to their lowest offer so that you can have a figure to use as leverage at another dealership

a) Restate your offer

b) State their offer

c) Gather up your keys, zip up your jacket and ask them if they can do better.

As an example, consider that your minimum is 25,000 and your maximum is 30,000.

You offer 25,000.

They counter at 29,000

You say "I'm looking to pay 25,000 for this car that I'm not too crazy about to begin with. You're offering it at 29,000 out the door right? I'll keep it in mind. Can you do any better than that? Maybe we can do business today."

Usually, this will send the salesperson back to her manager. Sometimes they will return with a lower quote, sometimes not.

The formula here is simple. Keep repeating the script above until the dealership will go no further. At that point, thank them and walk away.

The idea is to hang tough.

This is not the end of negotiations with this dealership. Any well run dealership will follow up with you by phone. Of that you can be sure! Usually this takes place within 48 hours of your visit.

When they call, you'll want to follow the script above and see if they will move on their price. If they do not, you can be fairly sure that this is their best price. You may call them back the next day with a counter offer. There are a number of reasons why they settle on a certain figure. Chief among these is the fact I stated earlier: They know a sucker will come along soon enough and pay the sticker price on the 7 year payment plan.

Now you've left the dealership and you're waiting on a phone call. This is the time to do your Internet shopping. This is amazingly easy. Go back to the manufacturer's online inventory; find a similar car at another dealership and call. When you do so, quote the price you got from your showroom visit, the dealership and the name of the salesperson. Here's a great script:

"I'm interested in stock # 9999 the blue Plymouth Duster, I just got a quote from Jimmy at Perk's Plymouth for 9,000 can you beat it?"

After a talk with a manager and a callback, you'll often find that they'll offer you a competitive price.

Do this a few more times at a few more dealerships. After getting your best price through the various Internet sales divisions, guess whom you'll call next? That's right! The dealership you originally visited. They may be a bit more willing to come down on their price now that they have some competition!

When you finally feel that you have a deal you can live with, you'll want to get a firm quote. Have them fax you the information with the VIN and an "out the door" price. Make SURE the fax states that the price is an OTD price.

When you've completed these steps, you're ready to purchase, but negotiations are not over yet. Remember what I mentioned earlier? Negotiations are never finished until you have a signed deal and the keys in your hands. Even though you may think you have a deal, the dealership may have other plans. They will generally not change the terms of the original deal, but in most cases, they will be strongly determined to squeeze some back-end money out of you. They will usually attempt a number of channels:

1. Financing
2. Extended warranties.
3. Ignoring your OTD request and attempting to pile on junk fees.

This is a very hard sell, so get ready. Your goal in this part of the negotiation process is to stand firm.

Let's begin with financing. If you've followed my advice to this point, you have your financing established and ready to go. You've also been quite ambiguous whether or not you will actually finance with the dealership. This basically created an invitation for them to sell you on their loan products. This is not a bad thing because by doing so, you've dangled a carrot in front of their noses to get the price you wanted. Now you have to let them down. Whether you do so gently or not is up to you. Here are a few approaches:

First, the polite let-down:

Salesperson: "How do you intend to pay for this?"

You: "What kind of rates can you offer"

Salesperson: "Fill out this credit application and I'll find out." (They almost always do this before quoting rates. If they happen to throw out some numbers first, just smile and say "no thanks")

You fill out the credit application, peruse the rates he returns with and then politely decline. He will counter, but you will stand firm. Keep in mind that by taking this route, you divulge a great deal of your personal information including your social security number, and have a credit check entered into your credit history.

An alternative is to decline right off the bat and notify the salesperson that you've arranged your own financing. You can say: "No thanks, I have a check here from "InterLoan" I'll use it to cover the full amount"

At this point, you'll have a very unhappy salesperson on your hands, but in most cases, they will begrudgingly proceed with the deal. An unscrupulous salesperson may attempt to shut it down. This is usually accompanied by an excuse such as "I'm sorry, but we just realized that another customer already placed a deposit on this car. This is entirely our fault. We shouldn't have even shown the car to you. Can we offer you the same deal on another vehicle?"

If this ever happens, you must insist on closing the deal on that car at the offered price or you will be in touch with your lawyer. You must be tough here.

Sometimes a dealership will attempt to override your resistance to the credit application by slipping it to you with an excuse in hand. I've heard this one before: "The Department of Homeland Security requires you to give us your social security number and fill out the C1 form". In reality, they're handing you a credit application. This seems to be a new scam among some car dealerships. While it is true that according to Office of Foreign Assets Control (a department of the US Treasury) a dealership can get into trouble when doing business with a known terrorism suspect, they do NOT need you to fill out a credit application to clear you for the purchase. A simple name search in the OFAC database is sufficient.
(http://www.ustreas.gov/offices/enforcement/ofac/)

In case your dealership attempts this scam, you must state in no uncertain terms that this is a lie that you will ignore. The one time I encountered this, I quickly shut this down by simply saying "I'm very familiar with the department of homeland security, please don't embarrass yourself further. I'm going to write you a check for the full amount now. Let's do business." The fact that my familiarity with the Department of Homeland Security came from my extensive experience reading newspapers was none of their business.

A dealership may also seek backend money from you through the sale of an extended warranty. The sales pitch here may be lengthy and elaborate. The key to dealing with this is to determine beforehand whether you want the extended warranty and what kind of warranty you want. Use the negotiation principles explained earlier to arrive at your price. If you determine that you do not want a warranty, simply decline each offer and argument until you reach the point where politeness is getting you nowhere. Flatly decline at this point and ask for the keys. It is a reasonable response to rude high-pressure tactics.

If the dealership ever attempts to add junk fees to an "out the door" price, you must argue forcefully that will not tolerate this behavior. Again, mention of a lawyer, or television consumer advocate can do wonders.

Step 7: Closing the deal

In theory, this step should entail nothing more than writing a check and signing some paperwork. Don't take this step lightly. Keep these important points in mind:

1.   READ ALL PAPERWORK BACK AND FRONT – Make sure you're not signing something you'll regret.

2.   You may have to sign an arbitration agreement. This basically states that any dispute you may have with the dealership will go to arbitration rather than a court of law. If a dealership has this in it's paperwork pile, it will usually be non-negotiable. If you do not sign it you don't get the car. My personal opinion is that this is an unscrupulous practice but presents little risk to you when buying a new car. I would NEVER sign one of these when buying a used car. Use your best judgment. The decision is up to you.

Step 8: Delivery

This is where the dealership presents you with the keys and instructs you on the use of each of the features of the car. You will likely find that the dealership personnel have changed their attitude at this point. In most cases, they've become amicable. This is because the battle is over. You can relax now. Make good use of this portion by asking questions to get a full understanding of your new vehicle.

Step 9: The Drive Home

Play the radio loud and congratulate yourself. You're now the proud owner of a brand new car that was purchased at the lowest price possible!

Conclusion

There are a few things I hope I've given you in this book.

The first is a great price on a great car!

The next is an understanding of the complexity of the car business. Always keep that in mind when you visit a car dealership. These people work 8-14 hours per day to maximize their profit at your expense. The average person, in comparison, will purchase a new car only a few times in a lifetime. To do battle on this battlefield, you need information. Let friends and relative know what you know. They need this information too. When more people have an understanding of the car business, fewer people will be taken advantage of.

Finally, I hope I've given you insight into how negotiations work in general. The winner is ALWAYS the person who can walk away from the deal. The loser is ALWAYS the person who wants the deal more. Dealerships put you in the losing position by whetting your appetite then wearing you down until you are desperate. Desperation, in this case is really silly if you think about it since a new car with the same features can be found at almost any dealership. There are no "once in a lifetime" opportunities. This same negotiating principle applies to so many areas in life: Buying a home, business contracts, employment and some even say dating!

Think about how many of the guiding principles apply to every day situations. Here are some:

- Don't be a payment buyer. Resist the temptation when the salesperson tells you that he can "get you in this (fill in the blank) for only $249 per month"

- Do your research ahead of time.
- Be friendly.
- Be persistent.
- Stay in control of the process.
- Don't let your emotions get the best of you.
- Be patient
- Never let on how much you really like the (fill in the blank!)
- Never believe anything a salesperson tells you – verify everything.
- Your Starting price is much lower than your maximum price.
- The only offer you negotiate on is an "Out the door price" or O.T.D.

Keep that in mind as you go forward in life. Remain ambivalent!

Best fortunes and great deals!

Appendix A - Forms

Maximum Negotiated Price

Make:_____

Model:_____

Trim Package:_____

Invoice Price : _____.__

Plus (+)

Tax: _____.__

Plus (+)

DMV: _____.__

Minus (-)

Rebate: _____.__

Maximum Negotiated Price: _____.__

Minimum Negotiated Price

Make:_____

Model:_____

Trim Package:_____

Invoice Price : _____.__

Plus (+)

Tax: _____.__

Plus (+)

DMV: _____.__

Minus (-)

Rebate: _____.__

Minus(-)

Dealer Cash: _____.__

Minus(-)

Dealer Holdback: _____.__

Minimum Negotiated Price: _____.__

Appendix B - Resources

Financing

http://financial.wellsfargo.com

www.lendingtree.com

www.bankrate.com

http://www.ustreas.gov/offices/enforcement/ofac/

Used/New car price references

www.edmunds.com

www.kbb.com

Selling your used car

www.craigslist.com

www.carmax.com

http://pages.ebay.com/securitycenter/

www.ingramcontent.com/pod-product-compliance
Lightning Source LLC
Chambersburg PA
CBHW051717040426
42446CB00008B/938